Praise for **Wandering**
Readers are talking about:

One of the best memoirs I've read in a long time!!

Sharon Kreider weaves two poignant stories: one about childhood abuse and family neglect and the other about finding refuge and purpose in exploring the world. She writes with sincerity and humility about trekking through the Himalayas and living at ashrams in India. The resulting story is a wonderful portrait of a wounded yet courageous young woman determined to find her place in the world. It's authentic and not self-congratulatory, as many of these types of travelogue/self-discovery memoirs can become. I found her narrative awe-inspiring and courageous.

I read a lot and was impressed with this book. The author did an amazing job of drawing you into the travel experience through rich descriptions of each place's tastes, smells, and feel. I feel like I have been to all the locations talked about. Well done!

Sharon is a wonderful writer. I had a hard time putting the book down. It was fascinating and inspirational.

Sharon Kreider's open and honest account of her journey is not just captivating; it's life-changing. Her beautifully written descriptions of places, people, and emotions make you feel like you're part of the experience. This tender and heartwarming memoir doesn't just touch your soul; it challenges your beliefs and leaves you with a renewed belief in your own courage to face life's challenges.

A tender story that captivates from the first page. Sharon is an incredible writer and has lived a life that deserves to be shared. Highly recommend!

A woman's journey through despair, love, healing, and travel! It is a very well-told memoir that makes you wonder how she survived. Ms. Kreider has a gift for describing heart-wrenching episodes in a way that draws the reader to her humanity without being maudlin or voyeuristic. Her second book is easy to read; a rich, rewarding experience that I highly recommend.

Wandering by Sharon Kreider captures an exquisite tale of courage, love, and adventure! The vivid descriptions left me breathless as if I were with her in 1977 in India and Nepal! It scratches that perfect wanderlust itch of an excellent travel memoir. For those who want to explore, experience, and be swept away, you will not be disappointed with picking up Wandering! This is a story you will come back to think about and appreciate long after the last page has been read.

Sharon Kreider doesn't just tell you about her journeys; she takes you with her. With stunning landscapes, spicy aromas, piquant flavors, sweltering heat, numbing cold, and connections both heartbreaking and heartwarming, "Wandering" was an amazing adventure that no reader will forget.

Loved this book! Will be re-reading!

This is a must-read! Check it out.

Capturing a pre-internet era and the trekking journey of a young woman in search of place and self, **Wandering... A Long Way Past the Past** is a powerful recreation of a bygone world of innocence and wonder. It is more than a notch above contemporary travelogue memoirs, making for a vivid read that libraries will want to consider for its lasting value.

Praise for **Sylvie**
Readers are talking about:

Descriptive language paints a great story picture and provides incredible details of characters and emotions. I love how the author focused each chapter on a specific character, providing each individual's perspective of reality. Although **Sylvie's** story is sad, it reveals crucial insights we all can relate to. One person never really knows the whole truth, especially if isolated from another's reality.

This excellent book reminds us what it truly means to be human, to feel grief, to have doubts, and to have hope despite it all.

It's a riveting story! I found it difficult to put it down. The story offers a look into the internal emotional struggles that aren't visible on the outside. It is not only fascinating but also makes me more aware of our strengths and weaknesses and of accepting others for who they are.

It didn't take me long to become engrossed in this book! It seemed more like non-fiction, especially the mourning period after losing a child. I lost my daughter in a car accident when she was 19. The horrible mourning process was described perfectly. The hardest part was waking up every morning for several years feeling normal, then remembering that she was dead. It was a never-ending nightmare. I could relate so much to Sylvie's life and all the suffering she went through making friends and feeling lonely and outcast. My daughter went through some of the same things. It's so sad! Children can be so cruel! Every parent should be aware of the sadness other children go through and talk to their children. This is happening in schools all over America.

Sylvie is a compelling novel that investigates family relationships and bullying. The character development is excellent, and I found it difficult to put the book down, anxious to know what would happen next in Sylvie's life. It is a must-read for parents of pre-teens and early teens.

A riveting tale of love and loss.

I loved the author's nature descriptions, which appealed to all the senses, and her poetry, which evoked a Zen-like quality. I'm so glad I read this remarkable book and look forward to hosting it for our book club.

Sharon does a fantastic job humanizing a topic that we often look at as taboo. By presenting us with characters we can relate to or recognize, we get wrapped into the story and invested in the personalities and their outcomes (and maybe hollering at them for their decisions/actions, sometimes).

It has it all! I could not put it down.

Humans and their emotions are complicated and intertwined with those around them. Through **Sylvie,** Sharon clarifies these connections and explains how our actions, as minor as we may see them when stacked, may have a bigger and more significant impact.

If you have or work with kids or teens, this is a must-read. It is also a must-read if you enjoy a well-crafted story!

Incredible story, character development, and beautiful descriptive narrative. This is a beautiful, tender story of love and loss with deep emotional depth.

This book is simultaneously heartwarming and heart-wrenching, taking the reader on an emotional journey that is not to be missed!

This book is a page-turner and heartbreaker. Wonderfully written and deep in meaning.

Silver Tip
poems

Also, by Sharon Kreider

Sylvie

Wandering

Silver Tip
poems

Sharon Kreider

**Silver Tip
poems**

© 2024 by Sharon Kreider.
All Rights Reserved.

All rights reserved, including the right to reproduce this book
or portions thereof in any form whatsoever.

Editor: Meg Ryan
Cover, Interior Design, and eBook conversion:
Rebecca Finkel, F+P Graphic Design, FPGD.com

Books may be purchased in quantity by contacting
Gray Wolf Books / www.graywolfbooks.com

Library of Congress Control Number: 2024911770

Paperback: 978-1-7372393-7-6
eBook: 978-1-7372393-8-3

Poetry | Nature | Ecopoetry | Love

For Rea

Silver Tip
poems

Sharon Kreider

In my early college years, my favorite poet was Bashō. I accidentally discovered his poetry when browsing a bookstore for travel tips. I didn't have much money, so I was looking for something inexpensive and noticed a small Penguin Classic called *Bashō: The Narrow Road to the Deep North and Other Travel Sketches*. At the time, I thought the paperback might have some insight into how I might accomplish my dream of touring the world. The book didn't have much traveling advice, but it gave me something far more valuable.

The book tells the story of the respected Japanese poet Bashō through his remarkable contribution to the shortest form of Japanese poetry called haiku. Haiku, or *hokku* as it was called when Bashō lived (1644-1694), consists of seventeen syllables divided into three sections of five-seven-five. The haiku he created to describe the world around him are nothing short of astonishing, and I find more meaning in them every time I read one.

On the surface, haiku are descriptive, but I think the best haiku suggest a simple symbolic quality, an expression that transcends the moment—something that gives us an *a-ha* flash that strengthens our connection to the natural world and holds a deeper meaning.

4 Silver Tip poems

Over the years, I've kept a journal, just a simple lined notebook, in which I've written hundreds of haiku trying to emulate Bashō and my connection to the natural world, especially when I need to express how wonderful living truly is. For me, there is comfort in the down-to-earth writing of haiku, a discipline in whole-heartedly committing to the moment, to capture the essence of now, to freefall into what is.

> snow falls quietly
>
> soft as dandelion heads
>
> blanketing my thoughts

> winter sun rises
>
> makes me wish for the brightest
>
> colors of summer

> love looks like white snow
>
> next to a blooming flower
>
> showing me the light

> just before sunrise
>
> as the sky begins to glow
>
> I remember you

Before I discovered Bashō, I spent hours reading *The Complete Poems of Emily Dickinson*, one of the best-selling and most revered poetry books of all time, alongside Henry David Thoreau's *On Walden Pond*. Thoreau, a complex man with many talents, spent much of his time living a simple life close to nature. Perhaps admiring the view from his window, a scarlet maple in fall, summer's purple clover, or the pristine white of winter. Jotting down his thoughts. Asserting his individuality.

 I, too, like to look out my window and appreciate a mist rising from the melting snow, ghostlike shapes meandering through the tall cedars and bare larches. Where harmony is found in the way a tree grows, and rain disappears once it falls onto a lake's surface. I, too, appreciate solitude and quiet hours in which to write, compose poems, and try my best to describe the moment, one word at a time.

The following contemporary poems are a collection of some of my favorites. They offer a window into my sense of self, using nature to create a strong image while keeping it as simple as possible and with no specific form.

An Afternoon in My Home

Outside smoke from nearby fires fills the air with dust and particles,

heat-surge like blackened coal. Out my window I see

another tree turning brown, the parched earth wildfire dry

gasping for breath, thirsty, almost desperate.

When I open the front door it's as if I am stepping

right into my kitchen oven, the porch boards too hot to stand

on without my flip-flops or socks.

A deer and her fawn find shade under a large cedar tree

munch on a patch of green grass in a yellowed pasture

while a hummingbird darts between lavender and coreopsis bushes

finding refuge in meager places of moisture and life.

I am out for ten minutes. Enough time to turn on the sprinkler, hopeful

my paltry attempt will provide relief to the few visiting animals and birds on my land, perhaps, summon the rain gods

to stop by long enough to give us all

a break from the unrelenting heat of a climate change
season we'll likely never forget.

Back inside, soft music drifts through my home and the air conditioner

keeps the temperature a luxurious 75 degrees

and remember for everything there is a season

a time for red-hot intense, sea-blue cool, ups and downs

time to sit in the middle of perfect possibility

or botched undertakings and time, lots of time

to cherish all that I love.

Alfa Romeo

Up and down ridges
eucalyptus kangaroo tracks
kookaburra calls a dead wombat
stepping in mud
from yesterday's thunderstorm
hail wind a downpour
so fierce I couldn't see
out the front window
of my son's 1988 Alfa Romeo
an old car carefully
refurbished only slightly
still running after 250,000 miles
deteriorating upholstery
a few funky smells
silently enduring the demands
complaining every now
and again a few creaks
moans and surprises
hard to start
a loose screw
on the floor not unlike
my tighter hips sore knees
forgetfulness the ache
in my lower back my sighs
remembering
1988

Alone

Beyond the burn pile, flanked
by tall cedars and three larch trees

a small track is hemmed
by stalwart weeds. On it I

run with my mouth open
in song. The wind in my hair

feels like forgetting and
remembering all at once:

how much I begged you
to buy this land for us

a forever place to grow old
rest relax find balance

ignore the passage of time
the inevitable. Not that

you might go first, that
I might be alone running

through our footpath, tears
streaming down my face.

Angel

The light pulls away from the trees

leaving them in shadow

A few stars rise above the hills

as a crescent moon

shines on newly fallen snow

Reminiscent of making snow angels

before

you became part of the night

Blacksmith Beach

No hurries no worries

dry hot sunny windy

sinking in the powder-like sand

a challenge to walk fast

each step like lifting weights

big ocean swells

from the quick efficient winds

pummeling off the sea

the glare of the sun

so strong my sunnies

don't quite do the trick

my thoughts settling into

a quieter rhythm

not as restless as my

yesterdays

Quiet Here

It's quiet here. The rain drips

off the roof, hits the deck.

The Japanese maple quivers

in the wind, its brown leaves

still holding on, not ready

to fall or be alone.

I am writing about you.

How I miss sitting side by side

by that tree, watching

the seasons change

from red to brown

from white to lime green

to new life

home to a flycatcher's nest

a bluebird song

laughter on a summer afternoon

sitting there, holding hands

sipping our morning coffee.

It's quiet here. The rain drips
off the roof, hits the deck.
The Japanese maple quivers
in the wind, a brown leaf
falls and touches the ground
without a sound.

The Quilt

I'd always thought of my mother as a seamstress—
the quilts she made with pride
turquoise blue squares mingled with scarlet reds
waterfalls splashed against mountain ridges
yellow circles stitched close to orange swirls
rosy pink wings resembling birds in flight
black on white on crimson cliffs
places she hoped to visit but never did
after years of mending, healing, suffering
now long gone, her ashes in the wind. All is past
except the last quilt she made
from the scraps of all the others
a thing of beauty really without a theme
just strips of glorious color
different shades of blue green purple
red yellow orange creamy whites midnight blacks
earthy browns embroidered in concert
as if related somehow, singing a lifetime of wishes
kept in a safe spot protected from the sun
from the passage of time, sealed and closed
like King Tut's tomb.

The Loft

It's a loft. The blinds are closed

to block the morning light so bright

it reflects off the computer screen

and fills the empty spaces. A loft

for writing poems, stories about

the past, of what-ifs, worlds

without borders, a place to drink

hot tea, ponder new ideas. Quiet

often in this place. A stack of books

thesauruses, files, newspaper clippings

magazine articles, an award. A refuge

from the rain-soaked shambles

of time, the snowdrift cupboards

of fame, fortune. Capturing an old lady's

laugh when she thinks she might

be young again and walk

in fields of silver and gold.

The Bond

In the woods I come upon a wild turkey

skittish and untrusting

fleeing here and there

clucking at me

trying to get me to follow

further away from a deep stream

where a possible nest

lay hidden from the sun

its cry reminding me of standing

near a sharp-edged cliff

and looking down onto treetops

brush, fallen logs, a river running madly

splashing over its banks

in a rush to get home

the ache in my belly rising to meet

my fear of falling

of no longer knowing whom to ask

what to ask

jumpy uneasy

hiding from the truth

of always wanting you

by my side

guiding me in the dark

in the light

with my choices

holding my hand

showing me the way

Talisman

The tiny moccasin with delicate

emerald green

and crimson red glass beads

carefully embroidered

on top and along the sides

rests in the palm of my hand

Found amongst a dozen human skeletons

in a cave on the west coast

of Vancouver Island

during a ten-day backpacking trip

along the rugged shoreline

Reminds me

to take time for empty hours

in my day and aimless rooms

in my life to be myself

and know I don't need to push the river

it flows by itself

Twilight

Wind blows through the trees
as twilight descends. Snowbanks
as high as my waist crunch
under my boots. The mountains
silhouetted in the distance seem
to lean in close as if to whisper
a blessing as darkness descends. One
by one, the stars come out, bright
then brighter, like lupine
in spring, small lavender buds, then magnificent
violet blooms. I hear a lone
coyote, then the hoot of a distant owl. A half-moon
peeps up behind the tallest spruce
creating fingers of light dancing on the snow.
My nose
tingles in the cold and I smile. Then walk
home to warmth and all I love.

Shelter

Not far from where I live

a grove of large hemlock

and cottonwood trees

Goliath wrinkles on rippled bark

nestle in a dark ravine

deeply rooted and tall

long ago missed by loggers

provide sanctuary

from snowflakes as big as

nickels and quarters

I take a lungful of air

gaze up at a tangled maze of branches

and wonder

if I hang out with them

long enough

could I too be

strong

still

silent

a giant in a shrinking world

Raku

Sashimi tuna salmon scallops

edamame sashimi rolls

grilled corn broccolini

zucchini flowers tenderloin skewers

teriyaki salmon best glass of wine

cocktails followed by pistachio

hazelnut mint gelato

heart full mind blown

together family one

I Forgive

The way he periodically

waltzed into my young life

and messed things up

The way he pretended

to be a father to a little girl

but really was only a stranger

And I forgive my hopeful heart

for always wanting him to be

a loving father who protected

and played silly games and sang

songs to satisfy my

incessant longing

For Mel

Freezing rain fell

covering everything

in a half-inch layer of ice

the day I found out

you took your last breath

impossible to go outside

for a walk. Roads paths sidewalks

slippery as a skating rink

impossible to believe

you, no longer here

the sound of your beautiful laugh

echoing in my heart. Remembering

sunny days sipping lattes

chatting about things you love

Paul, a daughter, two sons

dogs, more dogs, Greece

good food, flowers, dreams

compassion for others. Healing

the world one tender word

after another. Who knows

how many people you saved

hundreds, thousands

who are better because you lived

you cared you loved

you, a light in this world,

snuffed out too soon

yet not forgotten not dead

not gone but here

blooming in the present.

Only Light

The darkness of trees

guards my life

like the threadlike terrain

that covers the high rock

among wild hemlocks

and the magic

of the north

the wonder of silence

and shattered limbs

home to tiny creatures

and lime-green leaves

new flowers above

dark emerald moss below

in the sugary smell of decay

in the puddles and dribble

of rainwater

life decomposing

veiled in secrecy

like a looking glass

reflecting light

not shadow

only light, only light

Mountains in Summer

Always for most of my life now

I am in the mountains in summer

to hike up and down

steep slopes, wade blue-green rivers

avoid encounters with grizzlies

maneuver snowfields, sleep

under the stars. Fill my days

and nights with clean air, breathe

deep and long. Remember

who I am. The girl who wandered

over the West to become wild. To romp

through meadows full of bluebells

and fields of lavender lupine

laugh in the full moonlight

drink cold water from glacial streams

and gaze at far grass ridges

while lightning lit up the sky

joy coursing through my body.

Always for most of my life now

I am in the mountains in summer

to stare at exquisite peaks

and spacious valleys

watch bluebirds land on alder bushes

smell the rich scent of the earth

after a cloudburst. Feel raindrops

on my tongue. Touch

the soft tendrils of a larch

sway in a cool mountain breeze

and dance

with the ghost of history

implore the odds not to cascade down

through rocky ledges holding glaciers

but remain unchanged

stoically weather all things

with grace and grow rich

on the threat of death.

Bush Life

Kangaroos everywhere

mamas babies in pouches

silent elders, young bucks

kookaburras red ants termite hills

wind blowing through eucalyptus trees

rosellas warblers hot sun

flies mosquitoes quietude

Vision

Late morning, with my bundle

of dreams weighing heavy

as a blanket full of rain,

my fleeting stars

my pens dry of ink.

I close my eyes

cling to hope

cross my arms, nod

open my laptop

stare at the empty screen.

Shake my head

trust the movement

will loosen dust

and wait, with two closed fists

for the song to sing.

Perhaps

I know you are right
when you say
that nothing lasts forever.

Everything changing, shifting.

Sometimes morphing
into something unrecognizable,
like my face in the mirror.

I know you are right
when you say
we never know our time.

But I like to think we might
snowshoe our way into the night
side by side.

Find that spot deep in the woods
and sit quiet
under a Sitka spruce.

Counting our breaths
in tandem
until darkness arrives.

Sharon Kreider

Email Poem for Robyn

Hey Robyn, spent the last few days kayaking the St. Joe River near Lake Coeur d'Alene in North Idaho. A few men, talking at the campsite next to ours, kept remarking how the river should be reserved for fly fishermen who long for hours of uninterrupted casting in the eddies away from the swift current, not for kayakers wanting to float 'their beautiful river.' This time of year, the water runs at 3900 cubic feet per second compared to last year's 10,000, making it impossible to paddle then, logs quickly bobbing past, only to get jammed down the river. We put in just above Marble Creek and maneuvered a set of white-capped rapids before settling into the middle stream, the green water so clear you could see to the bottom. It didn't feel like we were going that fast, but when my eyes followed my oar into the water, the passing view of stones and the occasional rainbow trout was like watching a movie on fast forward. About halfway, we ferried onto a small pebble beach for a quick lunch before embarking again, the river less turbulent, kinder to my arms, straining to keep away from a sudden dip or the fast-moving cascades next to a bluff. On the last mile or so, the river softened considerably, still moving, of course, but quieter;

the grasses on the embankments swaying in the breeze –a million ballerinas reminding me of you dancing on the flat rocks near our lake camp, your eyes full of wonder. We didn't see other kayakers, only focused fishermen casting their lures and thousands of mayflies landing on the water's surface while trout leaped to catch them. It doesn't seem right that this river should be kept for only those wanting to catch fish, but I doubt I'll go next year. There are other rivers, lakes, and ponds to explore.

My Faith in You

with honor and loyalty

embellished

in your heart

like the old television series

Lassie,

I believe everything

you tell me

and though sometimes I should

know better

and not take you so seriously

maybe even laugh

let my fingers ruffle through

your hair

I can't help myself

for always believing

in you

the way your eyes mist

over when I recite

a recent poem

the kindness you show

to strangers

the love you shower

me with day after day

as we grow old and older

and older

and if you were to tell me

that there is indeed a place

where we will meet after death

I would believe you

I would believe you

as I've always done before

Dawn

Dawn breaks for no one

drifts over the hill

spills into my home

sneaks past the curtain

dances on the feather comforter

before flying on

to the forest

as the sun rises

promising a blue-sky day

Colors mingle

the world wakes

sunlight drops from branches

warms the earth

melts a spring frost

a bluebird sings

then two more

echo the joy

of a new day

Sunday Smells

of homemade donuts filled with jam

and sprinkled with icing sugar

so soft and yummy

my teeth sink through

until warm velvety pastry

touches the roof of my mouth

My grew-up-in-the-depression mother

always speaking less

seeming too quiet

smiles and stares down at her hands

she knows no other way

to show her heart

The Path

The path climbs, noises

fall away. Two hawks fly

overhead. To my right,

in a flowering laurel, a bluebird

eyes the terrain

as the wind lifts my hair.

When the path levels

I look down, the lake

in full view. A turquoise gem

amid grey-black rock,

lime-green larch, blue spruces

a cobalt sky.

Ahead, the path rolls

in undulating waves

of many colors. My steady

heartbeat in rhythm

with the nature of things

with the nature of you.

Hold On to Nothing

Sun drops below the cedars

moon comes along

and freezes the last red leaves

of a solitary maple

the light pulls away

into the shadows

as stars rise, glint

in the distance

a squirrel scampers

across a pile of dried grass

chirps and squeaks

dashes into its hole

as I stand in the dark

and let the threads

of silence weave

into my heart

Peter's Snow

It's white and swift and falls in sheets

covering the earth, obliterating

the tractor scars and the memory

of us laughing on the back deck

overjoyed to see you

after years away. We sat drinking

lemonade bathed in the light

of the late afternoon sun

a beautiful green sea of wild grasses

their feathery seed pods

swaying in the wind

back and forth

like a group of dancers twirling

Mozart playing

in the background.

Now I am alone

looking out the window at the distant hills

blanketed by layers of snow

white icing on a cake

cold as an Artic winter

remembering your smile that somehow

makes people want to dance

and comforts me

until spring

when I see you again.

Now I Do

I never thought I'd keep a file of kind words

or thoughtfulness

like collecting fireflies on a warm

summer night

in a jar to capture their magical

white light

flying around one another in seemingly

perfect harmony

the space between who we were then

and now

widening like a swollen glacial river

in spring

churning over boulders as big as houses

drowning sound

              How easily we drift apart

from our true nature

our common humanity

and write more compassionate words

thank my neighbor

anonymously pay for someone's coffee

let that mad driver in or pass

and be that person I always wanted to be

as the world spins around

and within us

Mooloolaba

Wave after wave

plummets the shoreline

white-tailed possums at night

kookaburra calls in the morning

by midday the sun

feels like I am in an oven

creamy white sand

too hot to walk on

without my flip-flops

salt crusts my upper lip

sand in my swimsuit bottoms

wave after wave

plummets the shoreline

lulls my thoughts

of old age, sickness, death

lulls my heart

of loss, what-ifs, what-now

lulls the throb

the constant tide

of not knowing

wave after wave

plummets the shoreline

quiets the ache

of my yesterdays.

For Natalie

With the hallmark of creativity

splashed

across your chest

like a Nobel Prize

I watch you create

pictures of surreal landscapes

and otherworldly shapes

Marvel when you lay a hand

against your breastbone

or forget to blink

your gaze fixed on the canvas

lighting up with beautiful

brushstrokes of marigold

indigo and dazzling reds

And when you tell me

that dinner can wait

or you might not be able to get

to those things I asked for

I let it go because

timelines and rules are meant

for us ordinary folk

Listen

The snow melts off the roof

drips in a steady stream

onto a north-facing gravel path

while a pileated woodpecker

hammers at a tall western Douglas fir

inspects for insects hidden within

looks up

calls to its mate

flies away

just as two deer flee

across the meadow

finding refuge in the shadows

just as my boots break

through a small puddle

my balance lost

I grab your hand

and lay my head on your chest

feeling the steady rhythm of your heart

beating in tandem with mine

Change

In the inland Northwest

cedar trees are dying

from the top down. Not enough

rain, too warm. Gray lichen

hangs from bare branches, fragile as tissue

the moss brown instead of emerald

clouds have not appeared

for over two months.

Wildfire smoke stings my eyes

makes me cough. I lick my parched lips

hungry for the sound of water,

for a storm.

Frost has not yet arrived

but the snowshoe hares living

in a nearby hallow

are turning white.

A flock of sparrows migrating

south stop to sit atop one

of the taller trees to look

for a quick snack. Finding none

they are suddenly gone

on their quest for a better place.

I watch them fly away

wishing for wings, feathers

to take me away from the heat

the change, to the past

when rivers flowed wild and full

blue and free.

Ode to Youth

Sometime in the morning light

it seemed I was climbing

a mountain

with my memory helping me up

but later

I see my hand

wrinkled with brown spots

and remember

the years

since that time

I raced up slopes

free, full of promise

eager for the summit

for my chest to seemingly burst

open like a thousand

migrating birds

leaving me speechless

as the wind played with

my hair

and sunlight danced

into my heart

For Angel

Eight delicate Calypso orchids

bloom under two large hemlock trees

their fragile pink petals open to the sky.

The soggy, damp moss underneath

yields to my soft touch

and the orchid's stems tremble slightly

in the breeze.

I remember you dying alone in a room

away from family and friends.

To take your last breath in this pandemic

by yourself

gives me no peace.

I watch the wildflowers for a moment longer

before leaving them untouched

to grow and die and live again.

Driving in Aotearoa

Undulating hills

the color of seagrass

a carpeted palette

of native trees

an eagle two hawks a heron

driving on the left

hugging the white line

curves potholes swerves

missing a perfect spot

for coffee and rest

carrying on through

the Big Smoke

then tiny villages

back to rolling hills

the color more evergreen

less lime to a quaint town

right smack in the middle

of the island

clean simple mowed lawns

an English feel

the sun sets

another day

Trees

Beneath the frozen ground

the ice thaws, melting the winter ice.

In the distance a raven calls

to its mate, sees a dead squirrel

on the road, hit by a logging truck

hauling trees from a nearby woodland

dead, too, from the chainsaw crew

with headphones on to drown

out the high-pitched screaming

of saws severing the mute cries

of an old-growth forest.

Caves Beach

Hot winds

sweep down from the north

over eucalyptus rainforest

koalas kangaroos kookaburras

green and red parrots

cockatoos rosellas

the heat-zapping air

drying out my T-shirt in seconds

my lips parched

stuck together

while I watch in horror

as old Ivy drops her front bumper

on the motorway going 110 kph

later we laugh over breakfast

toast trout spinach

poached eggs orange juice

admire the twinkle

in my son's eyes

grateful for another

beautiful sunny day

down under

and another

treasured family moment

just the five of us

Night

Sun drops below the trees

as darkness comes along

and freezes the melting snow

on the deck of my house.

In my room, I shake out

a blanket of regrets

and all the things I should've

said and done

and watch the moon

rise over a distant hill

spilling blue light

on the landscape of my past.

Over my shoulder

I see the threads of those

I love and catch a strand

clutching it hard, knowing

how insignificant my life is without

the enormous rope of their love.

In the Garden

The music plays

as rain falls outside

filling the potholes

and garden rows.

I doze in my chair

wondering when he might return

the thought warming my face

like soft petals of a flower

opening to the sun.

A sonata plays in the background

swells then gives way

to a gentle oboe melody

pulsing in the darkness.

A memory of dancing barefoot

in the muddy earth

with you by my side, a steady

downpour soaking our clothes.

No one noticed or cared

as we claimed each other

all the while listening

to the faraway notes

of a cello. Arms opened,

blinded by the joy.

Late Night

Late night with my bundle of dreams

weighing heavy in my limbs

I close my eyes

as the wheels slow, breath deepens

in silence, in solitude

not wanting time to pass

too quickly or to forget your beautiful

face all lit up with joy

the sky behind something Monet

might have painted

royal blue fading into soft lavender

into plum crimson into

night

Seasons Gone

I sit a moment

by the fireplace, outside rain, remember

snow, icicles forming off the roof

and those long nights, reading

how I picked up my mug of hot tea

blowing little ripples, breathing

in the peppermint and chamomile scent

thanking you for the kindness.

Somewhere out there

a bobcat sniffs around the old woodpiles

looking for a snowshoe hare

whose white fur will now turn brown

as it waits to eat the flowers

and romp in the summer air.

I close my eyes

rock in my chair

dream of seasons gone, remember

dancing in the meadow

your clear blue eyes

the color of glacial waters

and fall asleep, hopeful

when I wake

you might be there, sitting

with me by the fire, holding

my hand. Take my empty teacup

and refill it.

Love Is Love

Clear like water

smooth like glass

soft like rabbit fur

warm like the sun

close like now

quiet like the night

burning deep

burning strong

as seasons pass

pink bell-shaped flowers

burst open

leaves fall, snow then ice

song of a summer day

lawnmower rhythms

chainsaw drums

a child's laugh

rain on rain

wading where the willows

sweep over my teacup

and the wind blows

falling flowers

onto my lap

keeping safe

this love of mine and yours

Beyond

Above me, clouds. Beneath me, grass.

Ten thousand miles away, you sleep

as the world turns.   Below me,

small particles of sand silt clay rock

home to fungi and strange creatures and water

then bedrock and further still, mantle

before super-hot molten core.

All day, I think of you, my thoughts

like snowflakes falling on water

as the world turns.   Above me, stars.

Beneath me, living things who

love the night, forage for food

find a mate.   Below me, connected

to water, to the Rainbow Serpent,

to the great life giver and you.   Ten thousand

miles away, I sleep.

Spring

Five mauve crocuses bloom

between a pink azalea and two

lime green fiddlehead ferns. A violet

swallow lands on a fence searching

for a home while his partner

scolds him for taking his time

just as a lean cat slinks liquidly

around the corner. They eye each other

for a moment before the birds fly off.

So easily they leave danger. So easily

the cat pretends not to care. How familiar

it is to feel strange as the sky blurs.

A drop, then a few more, tasting

saltier than the sea we splashed in not

long ago. The cat now curled

in a ball near my feet.

Night Rose

When evening comes

I put the kettle on

make tea and wait

in a quiet house

while outside

a touch of rose clings

to a few drifting clouds

a crescent moon

and two stars

the door opens

you touch my sleeve

and I reach out to grasp

your callused fingers

feel the warmth

the touch of happiness

but nothing's there

Into Obscurity

Welcome me if you want

as the ambassador of a love

who knows sacrifice

and does not mind showing

the world

vulnerability and weakness

both shunned by

better people than I

and beg for peace

in the empty streets

and litter-filled highways

of my life while

banging into walls

taking up the final

threads of my life

between my teeth

hear a million hooting blood vessels

and wait for a mothlike adoration

which will not come

letting go of my terrible pride

so I won't cry from the grave

or stammer in the earth

but continue to grow flowers

Murrays Beach

I close my eyes

on the fine frosted quartz sand

where eucalyptus trees border the sea

for miles uninterrupted

next to water so clear

I can see

my reflection when I swim

amidst the seagrass

swaying to a timeless rhythm

by the full moon

living without me, dying

without me, while further out

a coral reef fights to breathe

give home to the broken-hearted

green turtle, minke whale

the giant oceanic manta ray

as a small crab climbs over

my toes. Stops for a moment

wondering where it might be

on the land of this earth

before it scrambles back

into the whitest sand in the world.

Alone.

For Rea

the north in autumn

a delicate changing world

full of soft wonder

on a frozen twig

light enters in a new way

shadow dances beneath

mindfully facing

the change from fall to winter

one breath at a time

I watch the moon rise

spilling clear light on the

landscape of my past

winter solitude

dense fog blankets the forest

silent, peaceful, still

snowflakes swirl around

gather in frozen clusters

not a sound is heard

fields of diamonds

glisten on the mountain slopes

perfect snowshoe day

twirling in the wind

I remember our life can

change in a heartbeat

small quiet rivers

begin their way down to meet

flowering green fields

hello sweet summer

sun shining and birds singing

light breezes and you

I love how summer

wraps its warm arms around me

the wild air the sun

turning not older

with years but newer every

moment every day

the courage to trust

love one more time and one more

time and love always

Acknowledgments

Thank you to the many poets who have inspired me over the years. Thank you for making this world a better place. Thank you for your unselfish and kindhearted dedication. Thank you for continuing to write and to publish. Your words are treasured more than you know.

Thank you to all the wonderful teachers I've had the opportunity to study with. There are so many that I fear I might miss one of you if I start naming all of you. So, thank you again for your wisdom, critiques, and compassion.

Thank you, Meg Ryan, editor, for your guidance and careful review of my poems. Thank you, Rebecca Finkel, book designer, for again helping me create a book cover and putting your special touch on the interior.

Thank you, Peter, Natalie, and Rea. Your love and support mean everything. Thank you, Rea, for being my biggest cheerleader. I love you.

And a special thank you to the natural world for continuing to be the source of my inspiration—the trees, flowers, plants, birds, animals, forests, mountains, sky, and all those things wild and free.

Bestselling author Sharon Kreider, a former mental health therapist turned writer, weaves the emotional and psychological fabric of the human condition into her writing and prose to help shed light on many relevant issues facing society today—its conflicts, tragedies, and windows of hope —something her life has mirrored.

Born and raised in a small northern Canadian town, she left home at an early age to travel the world, and eventually settled in Colorado where she penned her first book, **Sylvie** a women's fiction novel examining a family's love for one another, acceptance, and letting go. The siren call of the Pacific Northwest lured her to a new writing home on several acres of wild, natural land to live a quieter life with her husband.

Sharon's second book, **Wandering ... A Long Way Past the Past,** is a remarkable travel memoir. It is an exceptional account of courage, love, overcoming adversity, and forgiveness, spanning her three-year solo adventure from Canada to Asia in the late 1970s.

When Sharon is not writing, you can find her hiking the hills or kayaking the lake near her home in summer, cross-country skiing in winter, and as a long-time yoga instructor, teaching a yoga class from time to time. She lives a quiet life with her husband in the Pacific Northwest.

Sylvie is a tender, poignant novel examining a family's love for one another, acceptance, and letting go. Set in the Colorado mountains, it reveals the secrets and lies surrounding what appears to be the perfect family. Exploring the delicate threads binding a family together, we learn how an unexpected tragedy can unravel everything—and how they find hope, inspiration, and forgiveness to continue.

Readers will glean a peek into the mind and moods of a young woman struggling with choices and feeling unloved for most of her life. It's a must-read for grief groups, providing useful, understandable insight for parents and siblings of family members suffering the consequences of coping with unexpressed trauma.

It was the late 1970s …

… a time when mobiles, the internet, and more modern modes of touring were non-existent. It was a time when best-selling author Sharon Kreider embarked on her three-year solo adventure from her remote hometown in Canada to Asia.

Through her eyes, her experiences, and her words, you will discover:

- Majestic Nepal before the rest of the world did.
- The colors of India and rivers of love that flow through it.
- Goa and the most beautiful beach in the world.
- How the Middle East evoked questions: What am I doing? Where am I going? Who am I?

Wandering is a remarkable travel memoir; an exceptional account of courage, love, overcoming adversity, and forgiveness. It is a book of experiences, opening a window with a palette of words that enhance mouth-dropping scenic beauty, fearless friendships, and OMG happenings. You will not want to put the book down until you have read the last page.

www.ingramcontent.com/pod-product-compliance
Lightning Source LLC
Chambersburg PA
CBHW060617080526
44585CB00013B/863